TO

_____

FROM

FAMILY
CHRISTIAN
PRESS

FIRST CUP
DEVOTIONS

FOR
COUPLES

Printed in the United States of America

FIRST CUP
DEVOTIONS

FOR
COUPLES

TABLE OF CONTENTS

INTRODUCTION:
FIRST THINGS FIRST

How do you and your spouse begin the day? Do you awaken early enough to enjoy a few quiet moments together, or are you one of those couples who sleep until the last possible minute, leaving no time to invest in matters of the heart and soul? If you and your mate form the habit of getting up early—if both of you start the day by spending a few quiet moments with each other and with God—your marriage will be blessed. The fabric of your marriage is woven together with the threads of habit. And no habit is more important to your family's spiritual health than the habit of daily prayer and devotion to your Creator.

This book contains devotional readings that are intended to set the tone for the rest of your day. The text is divided into 30 chapters, one for each day of the month. Each chapter contains a brief essay, Bible verses, quotations, and a prayer, all of which can help you and your spouse focus on the blessings and opportunities that God has placed before you.

During the next 30 days, please try this experiment: Read one chapter each morning with your first cup of coffee—then discuss the devotional reading with your spouse. This simple act of "talking things over" will be helpful to both of you.

Your daily devotional time can be habit-forming, and should be. And, the first few minutes of each day are invaluable. So do yourself and your family a favor: start each day with God—He deserves no less, and neither, for that matter, do you.

IT ALL STARTS WITH GOD

No one has ever seen God.
But if we love each other, God lives in us,
and his love has been brought to
full expression through us.

1 JOHN 4:12 NLT

Do you and your spouse put God first in your marriage? Or do you allow yourselves to be hijacked by the inevitable obligations and distractions of 21st-century life? When you and your beloved allow Christ to reign over your lives and your marriage, your household will be eternally blessed.

God loved this world so much that He sent His Son to save it. And now only one real question remains: what will you and yours do in response to God's love? The answer should be obvious: You must put God first in every aspect of your lives, including your marriage.

God is with you always, listening to your thoughts and prayers, watching over your every move. As the demands of everyday life weigh down upon you, you may be tempted to ignore God's presence or—worse yet—to rebel against His commandments. But, when you quiet yourself and acknowledge His presence, God touches your heart and restores your spirits.

At this very moment, God is seeking to work in you and through you. So why not let Him do it right now?

God's love is measureless. It is more: it is boundless.
It has no bounds because it is not a thing
but a facet of the essential nature of God.
His love is something he is, and because he is
infinite, that love can enfold the whole created
world in itself and have room for ten thousand times
ten thousand worlds beside.

A. W. TOZER

Get yourself into the presence of the loving Father.
Just place yourself before Him, and look up
into His face; think of His love, His wonderful,
tender, pitying love.

ANDREW MURRAY

Everything I possess of any worth is
a direct product of God's love.

BETH MOORE

Though our feelings come and go,
God's love for us does not.

C. S. LEWIS

MORE FROM GOD'S WORD

*And we have known and believed the love
that God has for us. God is love, and he who
abides in love abides in God, and God in him.*

1 JOHN 4:16 NKJV

We love Him because He first loved us.

1 JOHN 4:19 NKJV

TODAY, WE WILL THINK ABOUT . . .

Ways that we can glorify God by
placing Him first in our marriage.

A PRAYER TO START OUR DAY

Dear Heavenly Father, You have blessed us with
a love that is infinite and eternal. In response to
Your gifts, let us be loving servants, Father,
and let us demonstrate our faith by placing You
first in our marriage *and* in every other
aspect of our lives. ~Amen

AND THE GREATEST OF THESE . . .

NOW THESE THREE REMAIN:
FAITH, HOPE, AND LOVE.
BUT THE GREATEST OF THESE IS LOVE.

1 CORINTHIANS 13:13 HCSB

The familiar words of 1st Corinthians 13 remind us of the importance of love. Faith is important, of course. So, too, is hope. But love is more important still.

Christ showed His love for us on the cross, and, as Christians, we are called upon to return Christ's love by sharing it. We are commanded (not advised, not encouraged . . . commanded!) to love one another just as Christ loved us (John 13:34). That's a tall order, but as Christians, we are obligated to follow it.

Sometimes love is easy (puppies and sleeping children come to mind) and sometimes love is hard (imperfect spouses come to mind). But God's Word is clear: We are to love *all* our family members, friends, and neighbors, not just the ones who seem most lovable. So today, take time to share Christ's love by word and by example. And the greatest of these is, of course, example.

For love to be true, it sometimes has to be velvet
and sometimes it has to be steel.

CHARLES STANLEY

Real love has staying power.
Authentic love is tough love.
It refuses to look for ways to run away.
It always opts for working through.

CHARLES SWINDOLL

A man and woman should choose each other for life
for the simple reason that a long life is
barely enough time for a man and woman to
understand each other, and to understand is to love.

GEORGE TRUETT

Love is the seed of all hope. It is the enticement to
trust, to risk, to try, and to go on.

GLORIA GAITHER

Lovers should see things in the ones they love
that others do not see.

ED YOUNG

MORE FROM GOD'S WORD

Beloved, if God so loved us,
we also ought to love one another.

1 JOHN 4:11 NKJV

Go after a life of love as if your life depended on it—
because it does. Give yourselves to the gifts
God gives you. Most of all, try to proclaim his truth.

1 CORINTHIANS 14:1 MSG

TODAY, WE WILL THINK ABOUT . . .

The importance of saying "I love you"
many times each day.

A PRAYER TO START OUR DAY

Dear Lord, You have given us the gift of love; let us
share that gift with others. And, keep us mindful
that the essence of love is not to receive it, but to
give it, today and forever. ~Amen

A LIFETIME OF LOVE . . . STARTING TODAY

THOUGH I SPEAK WITH THE TONGUES OF MEN
AND OF ANGELS, BUT HAVE NOT LOVE,
I HAVE BECOME SOUNDING BRASS
OR A CLANGING CYMBAL.

1 CORINTHIANS 13:1 NKJV

God's love for you is deeper and more profound than you can fathom. And now, precisely because you are a wondrous creation treasured by God, a question presents itself: What will you do in response to God's love? Will you ignore it or embrace it? Will you return it or neglect it? The decision, of course, is yours and yours alone.

When you and your spouse embrace God together, you are forever changed. When you embrace God's love, you feel differently about yourself, about your marriage, and about your family. When you embrace God's love—and when you do so together—you will share His message and you will obey His commandments.

When the two of you accept the Father's grace and share His love, you will be blessed here on earth and throughout all eternity. So, if you genuinely seek to build a marriage that will last, make God the centerpiece. When you do, your love will endure forever.

To love abundantly is to live abundantly,
and to love forever is to live forever.

HENRY DRUMMOND

The Bible tells us right up front that it is not good
for a man to be alone, that the Lord meant for us
to have a partner in life, and that without that
soul companion we're forever walking around,
looking for a missing part of ourselves. It's a truth
you may not fully understand until you find that
missing part and realize, for the first time, how you'd
lived so long with that empty feeling. They say
you don't know what you have until you lose it.
But I say: You don't know what you're missing
until you find it.

AL GREEN

The best use of life is love.
The best expression of love is time.
The best time to love is now.

RICK WARREN

In the presence of love, miracles happen.

ROBERT SCHULLER

MORE FROM GOD'S WORD

Love one another deeply, from the heart.

1 PETER 1:22 NIV

*May the Lord cause you to increase and abound in love
for one another, and for all people.*

1 THESSALONIANS 3:12 NASB

TODAY, WE WILL THINK ABOUT . . .

Creative ways to demonstrate the love
that we feel in our hearts.

A PRAYER TO START OUR DAY

Dear Lord, You have given us the gift of eternal
love; let us share that gift with each other and
with the world. Help us, Father, to show kindness to
those who cross our path, and let us show tenderness
and unfailing love to our family and friends.
Make us generous with words of encouragement and
praise. And, help us always to reflect the love that
Christ has given us, so that through us,
others might find Him. ~Amen

THE POWER OF COOPERATION

A KINGDOM THAT IS DIVIDED
CANNOT CONTINUE,
AND A FAMILY THAT IS DIVIDED
CANNOT CONTINUE.

MARK 3:24-25 NCV

Have you and your mate learned the art of cooperation? If so, you have learned the wisdom of "give and take," not the foolishness of "me first." Cooperation is the art of compromising on many little things while keeping your eye on one big thing: your relationship.

Cooperative relationships flourish over time. But, whenever couples fail to cooperate with each other, they sow the seeds of dissatisfaction, frustration, and competition within their marriage. In such cases, marriage partners may find themselves engaged in an unwitting "contest" to receive their "fair share" from the relationship. These types of struggles inevitably create far more problems than they solve.

If you're like most of us, you're probably a little bit headstrong: you probably want most things done in a fashion resembling the popular song "My Way." But, if you are observant, you will notice that those people who always insist upon "my way or the highway" usually end up with "the highway."

A better strategy for all concerned (including you) is to abandon the search for "my way" and search instead for "our way." The best marriages are those in which both partners learn how to "give and take" . . . with both partners trying to give a little more than they take.

Being committed to one's mate is not a matter of demanding rights, but a matter of releasing rights.

CHARLES SWINDOLL

It matters that we should be true to one another, be loyal to what is a family—only a little family in the great Household, but still a family, with family love alive in it and action as a living bond.

AMY CARMICHAEL

Money can build or buy a house.
Add love to that, and you have a home.
Add God to that, and you have a temple.
You have "a little colony of the kingdom of heaven."

ANNE ORTLUND

The family that prays together, stays together.

ANONYMOUS

I like to think of my family as a big, beautiful patchwork quilt—each of us so different yet stitched together by love and life experiences.

BARBARA JOHNSON

MORE FROM GOD'S WORD

A constantly squabbling family disintegrates.

MARK 3:24 MSG

. . . these should learn first of all to put their religion into practice by caring for their own family . . . .

1 TIMOTHY 5:4 NIV

TODAY, WE WILL THINK ABOUT . . .

Ways that we can be more cooperative.

A PRAYER TO START OUR DAY

Dear Lord, so much more can be accomplished when we join together to fulfill our common goals and desires. As we seek to fulfill Your will for our lives, let us also join with others to accomplish Your greater good for our families, for our communities, for our nation, and for our world. ~Amen

THE WORDS YOU SPEAK TODAY

PLEASANT WORDS ARE A HONEYCOMB,
SWEET TO THE SOUL AND
HEALING TO THE BONES.

PROVERBS 16:24 NIV

All too often, we underestimate the importance of the words we speak. Whether we realize it or not, our words carry great weight and great power, especially when we are addressing our loved ones.

The Bible reminds us that "Reckless words pierce like a sword, but the tongue of the wise brings healing" (Proverbs 12:18 NIV). And Christ taught that "Out of the abundance of the heart the mouth speaks" (Matthew 12:34 NKJV).

Does the "abundance of your heart" produce a continuing flow of uplifting words for your loved one? And do you express those feelings many times each day? You should.

When you're angry, do you reign in your tongue? Proverbs 29:11 teaches, "A fool gives full vent to his anger, but a wise man keeps himself under control" (NIV).

So, if you'd like to build a better marriage—and if you'd like to keep building it day by day—think before you speak. Avoid angry outbursts. Refrain from constant criticism. Terminate tantrums. Negate negativism. Cease from being cynical. Instead, use Christ as your guide, and speak words of encouragement, hope, praise, and, above all, love—and speak them often.

In all your deeds and words, you should look on Jesus as your model, whether you are keeping silence or speaking, whether you are alone or with others.

ST. BONAVENTURE

We will always experience regret when we live for the moment and do not weigh our words and deeds before we give them life.

LISA BEVERE

The battle of the tongue is won not in the mouth, but in the heart.

ANNIE CHAPMAN

Fill the heart with the love of Christ so that only truth and purity can come out of the mouth.

WARREN WIERSBE

Perhaps we have been guilty of speaking against someone and have not realized how it may have hurt them. Then when someone speaks against us, we suddenly realize how deeply such words hurt, and we become sensitive to what we have done.

THEODORE EPP

MORE FROM GOD'S WORD

He put a new song in my mouth, a hymn of praise
to our God. Many will see and fear and
put their trust in the LORD.

PSALM 40:3 NIV

May the words of my mouth and the meditation
of my heart be pleasing in your sight, O LORD,
my Rock and my Redeemer.

PSALM 19:14 NIV

TODAY, WE WILL THINK ABOUT . . .

The importance of measuring our words carefully,
especially when we're angry.

A PRAYER TO START OUR DAY

Dear Lord, make our words pleasing to You.
Let us be a source of encouragement to each other
as we share a message of faith and assurance
with the world. Today, we will honor You, Father, by
choosing our words carefully, thoughtfully,
and lovingly. ~Amen

ATTITUDE MATTERS

AND NOW, DEAR BROTHERS AND SISTERS,
LET ME SAY ONE MORE THING AS I CLOSE
THIS LETTER. FIX YOUR THOUGHTS ON
WHAT IS TRUE AND HONORABLE AND RIGHT.
THINK ABOUT THINGS THAT ARE
PURE AND LOVELY AND ADMIRABLE.
THINK ABOUT THINGS THAT ARE EXCELLENT
AND WORTHY OF PRAISE.

PHILIPPIANS 4:8 NLT

Christian marriage should be cause for celebration, but sometimes we don't feel much like celebrating. In fact, when the weight of the world seems to bear down upon our shoulders, celebration may be the last thing on our minds . . . but it shouldn't be. As God's children, we are all blessed beyond measure on good days and bad. This day is a non-renewable resource—once it's gone, it's gone forever. We should give thanks for this day while using it for the glory of God.

What will be your attitude today? Will you be fearful, angry, bored, or worried? Will you infect your marriage with the twin blights of cynicism and bitterness? Are you a person who celebrates your life and your marriage? Hopefully so! After all, God has richly blessed you, and He wants you to rejoice in His gifts. But, God will not force His joy upon you; you must claim it for yourself.

So today, and every day hereafter, celebrate the life that God has given you. Think optimistically about yourself, your marriage, your family, and your future. Give thanks to the One who has given you everything, and trust in your heart that He wants to give you so much more.

The purity of motive determines
the quality of action.

OSWALD CHAMBERS

Whenever a negative thought concerning
your personal power comes to mind, deliberately
voice a positive thought to cancel it out.

NORMAN VINCENT PEALE

Why did the achievers overcome problems while
others were overwhelmed by theirs? Achievers
refused to hold on to the common excuses for
failure. They turned their stumbling blocks into
stepping stones. They realized that they
couldn't determine every circumstance in life
but they could determine their choice of attitude
towards every circumstance.

JOHN MAXWELL

The things we think are the things that feed
our souls. If we think on pure and lovely things, we
shall grow pure and lovely like them;
and the converse is equally true.

HANNAH WHITALL SMITH

MORE FROM GOD'S WORD

*A miserable heart means a miserable life;
a cheerful heart fills the day with a song.*

PROVERBS 15:15 MSG

*Keep your eyes focused on what is right,
and look straight ahead to what is good.*

PROVERBS 4:25 NCV

TODAY, WE WILL THINK ABOUT . . .

The impact that our attitudes have upon each other
and upon the rest of our family.

A PRAYER TO START OUR DAY

Dear Lord, help us have attitudes that are pleasing
to You as we count our blessings today, tomorrow,
and every day. ~Amen

SHARING HOPES AND DREAMS

WITHOUT WAVERING,
LET US HOLD TIGHTLY TO THE HOPE
WE SAY WE HAVE, FOR GOD CAN BE
TRUSTED TO KEEP HIS PROMISE.

HEBREWS 10:23 NLT

Are you willing to share your hopes and dreams? And, are you willing to entertain the possibility that God has big plans in store for you and your spouse? Hopefully so. Yet sometimes, especially if you've recently experienced a life-altering disappointment, you may find it difficult to envision a brighter future for yourself or your family. If so, it's time to reconsider your own capabilities . . . and God's.

Your Heavenly Father created you and your loved ones with unique gifts and untapped talents; your job is to tap them. When you do, you'll begin to feel an increasing sense of confidence in yourself and in your future.

It takes courage to dream big dreams and even more courage to share them. You will discover that kind of courage when you do three things: accept the past, trust God to handle the future, and make the most of the time He has given you today. Nothing is too difficult for God, and no dreams are too big for Him—not even yours. So start living—and dreaming—accordingly.

Dreams are wonderful things to share. Have you shared yours lately? Hopefully so. But if you've been hesitant to give voice to your hopes and plans, remember this: dreaming works best when it's a team sport.

You cannot out-dream God.

JOHN ELDREDGE

Dreaming the dream of God is not for cowards.

JOEY JOHNSON

To make your dream come true,
you have to stay awake.

DENNIS SWANBERG

May your day be fashioned with joy, sprinkled
with dreams, and touched by the miracle of love.

BARBARA JOHNSON

The future lies all before us. Shall it only be
a slight advance upon what we usually do?
Ought it not to be a bound, a leap forward
to altitudes of endeavor and success
undreamed of before?

ANNIE ARMSTRONG

MORE FROM GOD'S WORD

*Live full lives, full in the fullness of God. God can do
anything, you know—far more than you could ever
imagine or guess or request in your wildest dreams!
He does it not by pushing us around but by working
within us, his Spirit deeply and gently within us.*

EPHESIANS 3:19-20 MSG

Where there is no vision, the people perish . . . .

PROVERBS 29:18 KJV

TODAY, WE WILL THINK ABOUT . . .

The importance of sharing our hopes and dreams.

A PRAYER TO START OUR DAY

Dear Lord, give us the courage to dream and
the faithfulness to trust in Your perfect plan.
When we are worried or weary, give us strength
for today and hope for tomorrow. Keep us mindful
of Your infinite love, Your healing power,
and Your glorious plans for us today, tomorrow,
and forever. ~Amen

FAMILY PRIORITIES

YOU MUST CHOOSE FOR YOURSELVES
TODAY WHOM YOU WILL SERVE . . .
AS FOR ME AND MY FAMILY,
WE WILL SERVE THE LORD.

JOSHUA 24:15 NCV

A loving family is a treasure from God. If God has blessed you with a close-knit, supportive clan, offer a word of thanks to your Creator because He has given you one of His most precious earthly possessions. Your obligation, in response to God's gift, is to treat your family in ways that are consistent with His commandments.

You live in a fast-paced, demanding world, a place where life can be difficult and pressures can be intense. As those pressures build, you may tend to focus so intently upon your obligations that you lose sight, albeit temporarily, of your spiritual and emotional needs (that's one reason why a regular daily devotional time is so important; it offers a badly-needed dose of perspective).

Even when the demands of everyday life are great, you must never forget that you have been entrusted with a profound responsibility: the responsibility of contributing to your family's emotional and spiritual well-being. It's a big job, but with God's help, you're up to the task.

When you place God squarely in the center of your family's life—when you worship Him, praise Him, trust Him, and love Him—then He will most certainly bless you and yours in ways that you could have scarcely imagined.

So the next time your family life becomes a little stressful, remember this: That little band of men, women, kids, and babies is a priceless treasure on temporary loan from the Father above. And it's your responsibility to praise God for that gift—and to act accordingly.

~ ~ ~ ~ ~ ~ ~

If I were starting my family over again,
I would give first priority to my wife and children,
not to my work.

RICHARD HALVERSON

You have heard about "quality time" and "quantity time." Your family needs both.

JIM GALLERY

As the first community to which a person is attached and the first authority under which a person learns to live, the family established society's most basic values.

CHARLES COLSON

MORE FROM GOD'S WORD

You can't go wrong when you love others.
When you add up everything in the law code,
the sum total is love. But make sure that you don't get so
absorbed and exhausted in taking care of all your
day-by-day obligations that you lose track of
the time and doze off, oblivious to God.

ROMANS 13:10-11 MSG

TODAY, WE WILL THINK ABOUT . . .

The importance of saying "yes" to our family even
if it means saying "no" to other obligations.

A PRAYER TO START OUR DAY

Dear Lord, we are part of Your family, and we praise
You for Your gifts and for Your love. You have also
blessed us with our own earthly family, and we pray
for them, that they might be protected and blessed
by You. Let us show love and acceptance for
our family, Lord, so that through us, they might
come to know You and to love You. ~Amen

THE WISDOM TO FORGIVE

BE KIND TO EACH OTHER, TENDERHEARTED,

FORGIVING ONE ANOTHER,

JUST AS GOD THROUGH CHRIST

HAS FORGIVEN YOU.

EPHESIANS 4:32 NLT

If we wish to build lasting relationships, we must learn how to forgive. Why? Because our loved ones are imperfect (as are we). How often must we forgive our spouses and our friends? More times than we can count; to do otherwise is to disobey God.

Are you easily frustrated by the inevitable imperfections of others? Are you easily angered? Do you sometimes hold on to feelings of bitterness and regret? If so, perhaps you need a refresher course in the art of forgiveness.

Perhaps granting forgiveness is hard for you. If so, you are not alone. Lasting forgiveness is often difficult to achieve—difficult but not impossible. Thankfully, with God's help, all things are possible, and that includes forgiveness. But even though God is willing to help, He expects you to do some of the work.

If there exists even one person, alive or dead, whom you have not forgiven (and that includes yourself and, of course, your spouse), follow God's commandment and His will for your life: forgive. Bitterness, anger, and regret are not part of God's plan for your life. Forgiveness is.

When God forgives, He forgets.
He buries our sins in the sea and puts a sign
on the shore saying, "No Fishing Allowed."

CORRIE TEN BOOM

Forgiveness is the precondition of love.

CATHERINE MARSHALL

Forgiveness does not mean the perpetrator goes free;
it means that the forgiver is free and that God will
justly deal with those who have caused pain.

CYNTHIA HEALD

Give me such love for God and
men as will blot out all hatred and bitterness.

DIETRICH BONHOEFFER

Every time we forgive others, deserving it or not,
we have a reminder of God's forgiveness.

FRANKLIN GRAHAM

MORE FROM GOD'S WORD

Why do you look at the speck of sawdust in your brother's eye and pay no attention to the plank in your own eye? How can you say to your brother, "Let me take the speck out of your eye," when all the time there is a plank in your own eye? You hypocrite, first take the plank out of your own eye, and then you will see clearly to remove the speck from your brother's eye.

MATTHEW 7:3-5 NIV

TODAY, WE WILL THINK ABOUT . . .

The need to make forgiveness a hallmark of our marriage.

A PRAYER TO START OUR DAY

Dear Lord, You command us to forgive each other quickly, thoroughly, and often. Keep us mindful, Father, that we are never fully liberated until we have been freed from the chains of anger— and that You offer us that freedom through Your Son Jesus. ~Amen

BUILDING ON A STRONG FOUNDATION

THEREFORE WHOEVER HEARS THESE SAYINGS OF MINE, AND DOES THEM, I WILL LIKEN HIM TO A WISE MAN WHO BUILT HIS HOUSE ON THE ROCK: AND THE RAIN DESCENDED, THE FLOODS CAME, AND THE WINDS BLEW AND BEAT ON THAT HOUSE; AND IT DID NOT FALL, FOR IT WAS FOUNDED ON THE ROCK.

MATTHEW 7:24-25 NKJV

Is your marriage built upon the firm foundation of God's love? Are you willing to obey God's commandments and to welcome His Son to rule your heart? Hopefully so. As you and your spouse grow in the love and knowledge of the Lord, you will also grow in your love for each other.

The 19th-century writer Hannah Whitall Smith observed, "The crucial question for each of us is this: What do you think of Jesus, and do you yet have a personal acquaintance with Him?" Indeed, the answer to that question determines the quality, the course, and the direction of our lives and our relationships.

The old familiar hymn begins, "What a friend we have in Jesus . . . ." No truer words were ever penned. Jesus is the sovereign friend and ultimate Savior of mankind. Christ showed enduring love for His believers by willingly sacrificing His own life so that we might have eternal life. Now, it is our turn to become His friend.

Let us love our Savior, praise Him, and share His message of salvation with our neighbors and with the world. When we do, we demonstrate that our acquaintance with the Master is not a passing fancy; it is, instead, the cornerstone and the touchstone of our lives.

The Lord Himself has laid the foundation
of His people's hopes. We must determine
if our hopes are built on this foundation.

C. H. SPURGEON

God is in control, and therefore in everything
I can give thanks, not because of the situation,
but because of the One who directs and
rules over it.

KAY ARTHUR

God is God. He knows what he is doing.
When you can't trace his hand, trust his heart.

MAX LUCADO

Sovereignty means that God alone ultimately has
the right to declare what creation should be.

STANLEY GRENZ

The Spirit of God is direct, authoritative,
the foundation of wisdom, life, and holiness.

ST. JOHN OF DAMASCUS

MORE FROM GOD'S WORD

The fundamental fact of existence is that this trust in God, this faith, is the firm foundation under everything that makes life worth living.

HEBREWS 11:1 MSG

God's solid foundation stands firm . . . .

2 TIMOTHY 2:19 NIV

TODAY, WE WILL THINK ABOUT . . .

The role that God should play in our marriage.

A PRAYER TO START OUR DAY

Dear Lord, You have promised never to leave us or forsake us. You are always with us, protecting us and encouraging us. Whatever this day may bring, we thank You for Your love and for Your strength. We will lean upon You, Father, this day and forever. ~Amen

A WILLINGNESS TO LISTEN

MY DEAR BROTHERS AND SISTERS,
BE QUICK TO LISTEN, SLOW TO SPEAK,
AND SLOW TO GET ANGRY.

JAMES 1:19 NLT

What a blessing it is when our loved ones genuinely seek to understand who we are and what we think. Just as we wish to be understood by others, so, too, should we seek to understand the hopes and dreams of our spouses and our family members.

Are you in the habit of listening to your mate? Do you listen carefully (not superficially), and do you take time to think about the things that you hear? If so, you're building a stronger marriage. But if you allow the obligations of everyday living to interfere with the communications you share with your spouse, it's time to reorder your priorities.

You live in a busy world, a place where it is all too easy to overlook the needs of others, but God's Word instructs you to do otherwise. In the Gospel of Matthew, Jesus declares, "In everything, therefore, treat people the same way you want them to treat you, for this is the Law and the Prophets" (Matthew 7:12 NASB). This is the Golden Rule, and it should govern your marriage.

Do you want your voice to be heard? Of course you do. So, in adherence with the Golden Rule, you should also let your spouse's voice be heard—by *you*.

Listening is loving.

ZIG ZIGLAR

The cliché is true: People don't care
what we know until they know we care.

RICK WARREN

The first duty of love is to listen.

PAUL TILLICH

The failure to listen might be the biggest hindrance
of all to marital communication.

ED YOUNG

The first service one owes to others in the fellowship
consists in listening to them. Just as love of God
begins in listening to His Word, so the beginning of
love for the brethren is learning to listen to them.
It is God's love for us that He not only gives us His
Word but lends us His ear. So it is His work that we
do for our brother when we learn to listen to him.

DIETRICH BONHOEFFER

MORE FROM GOD'S WORD

Listen to counsel and receive instruction
so that you may be wise in later life.
PROVERBS 19:20 HCSB

Wise people can also listen and learn.
PROVERBS 1:5 NCV

TODAY, WE WILL THINK ABOUT . . .

The importance of listening to each other.

A PRAYER TO START OUR DAY

Dear Lord, let us listen carefully to each other and
to You. When we listen, we learn. So, today and
every day, let us strive to understand each other
as we follow in the footsteps of Your Son. ~Amen

THE REWARDS
OF
RIGHTEOUSNESS

HE BLESSES THE HOME OF THE RIGHTEOUS.

PROVERBS 3:33 NIV

As you make plans for the upcoming day, make plans to live a life that will honor your family and your God.

A righteous life has many components: faith, honesty, generosity, love, kindness, humility, gratitude, and worship, to name but a few. If you seek to follow the steps of the One from Galilee, you must seek to live according to His commandments—you must, to the best of your abilities, live according to the principles contained in God's Holy Word.

Are you and your spouse striving to live righteously? If so, the two of you are building your marriage on a strong foundation. Do you seek God's peace for yourself and your family? Then here's what you must do: when you're faced with a difficult choice or a powerful temptation, you must seek God's counsel and trust the counsel He gives.

So, invite God into your heart and live according to His commandments. When you do, you and your family will be richly blessed.

Righteousness not only defines God,
but God defines righteousness.

BILL HYBELS

If we don't hunger and thirst after righteousness,
we'll become anemic and feel miserable in our
Christian experience.

FRANKLIN GRAHAM

We must appropriate the tender mercy of God
every day after conversion, or problems
quickly develop. We need his grace daily
in order to live a righteous life.

JIM CYMBALA

Holiness is not God's asking us to be "good";
it is an invitation to be "His."

LISA BEVERE

Trusting God is the bottom line of
Christian righteousness.

R. C. SPROUL

MORE FROM GOD'S WORD

*And now, children, stay with Christ. Live deeply
in Christ. Then we'll be ready for him when he appears,
ready to receive him with open arms, with no cause
for red-faced guilt or lame excuses when he arrives.
Once you're convinced that he is right and righteous,
you'll recognize that all who practice righteousness
are God's true children.*

1 JOHN 2:28-29 MSG

TODAY, WE WILL THINK ABOUT . . .

The importance of living lives that are
pleasing to God.

A PRAYER TO START OUR DAY

Dear Lord, this world is filled with so many
temptations, distractions, and frustrations.
When we turn our thoughts away from You and
Your Word, we suffer. But when we turn our
thoughts and prayers toward You and Your Son,
we are secure. Direct us, Father,
today and every day that we live. ~Amen

LESS IS MORE

DON'T BE OBSESSED WITH GETTING
MORE MATERIAL THINGS.
BE RELAXED WITH WHAT YOU HAVE.
HEBREWS 13:5 MSG

How important are our material possessions? Not as important as we might think. In the life of committed Christians, material possessions should play a rather small role, but sometimes, we allow the things that we own to take control of our lives. When we do, we suffer.

Too many marriages are weighted down by endless concerns about money and possessions. Too many couples mistakenly focus their thoughts and energies on newer cars, better clothes, and bigger houses. The results of these misplaced priorities are always unfortunate, and sometimes tragic.

Certainly we all need the basic necessities of life, but once we meet those needs for our families and ourselves, the piling up of possessions creates more problems than it solves. Our real riches are not of this world: we are never really rich until we are rich in spirit.

Do you find yourself wrapped up in the concerns of the material world? If so, it's time for you and your spouse to sit down and have a heart-to-heart talk about "stuff." When you do, you should reorder your priorities by turning away from materialism and back to God. Then, you can begin storing up riches that will endure throughout eternity: the spiritual kind.

Our ultimate aim in life is not to be healthy,
wealthy, prosperous, or problem free.
Our ultimate aim in life is to bring glory to God.

ANNE GRAHAM LOTZ

When we put people before possessions in our
hearts, we are sowing seeds of enduring satisfaction.

BEVERLY LAHAYE

He is no fool who gives what he cannot keep
to gain what he cannot lose.

JIM ELLIOT

When the apostle Paul met Christ, he realized
everything in his asset column was actually
a liability. He found that Christ was all he needed.

JOHN MACARTHUR

Faith in God will not get for you everything you
want, but it will get for you what God wants you to
have. The unbeliever does not need what he wants;
the Christian should want only what he needs.

VANCE HAVNER

MORE FROM GOD'S WORD

*No one can serve two masters. The person will hate
one master and love the other, or will follow one master
and refuse to follow the other. You cannot serve
both God and worldly riches.*

MATTHEW 6:24 NCV

TODAY, WE WILL THINK ABOUT . . .

The relative importance that we place upon
material possessions.

A PRAYER TO START OUR DAY

Lord, our greatest possession is our relationship
with You through Jesus Christ. You have promised
that, when we first seek Your kingdom and
Your righteousness, You will give us the things
we need. We will trust You completely, Lord,
for our needs, both material and spiritual,
this day and always. ~Amen

PRAYING TOGETHER

REJOICE ALWAYS! PRAY CONSTANTLY.
GIVE THANKS IN EVERYTHING,
FOR THIS IS GOD'S WILL FOR YOU
IN CHRIST JESUS.

1 THESSALONIANS 5:16-18 HCSB

Does your family pray together often, or just at church? Are you a little band of prayer warriors, or have you retreated from God's battlefield? Do you and yours pray only at mealtimes, or do you pray much more often than that? The answer to these questions will determine, to a surprising extent, the level of your family's spiritual health.

Jesus made it clear to His disciples: they should pray always. And so should you. Genuine, heartfelt prayer changes things, and it changes you. When you lift your heart to the Father, you open yourself to a never-ending source of divine wisdom and infinite love.

Your family's prayers are powerful. So, as you go about your daily activities, remember God's instructions: "Rejoice always! Pray constantly. Give thanks in everything, for this is God's will for you in Christ Jesus" (1 Thessalonians 5:16-18 HCSB). Start praying in the morning and keep praying until you fall off to sleep at night. And rest assured: God is always listening, and He *always* wants to hear from you *and* your family.

We must pray literally without ceasing, in every
occurrence and employment of our lives.
You know I mean that prayer of the heart which
is independent of place or situation, or which is,
rather, a habit of lifting up the heart to God,
as in a constant communication with Him.

ELIZABETH ANN SETON

It is impossible to overstate the need for prayer
in the fabric of family life.

JAMES DOBSON

The key to a blessed life is to have a listening heart
that longs to know what the Lord is saying.

JIM CYMBALA

In prayer it is better to have a heart without words
than words without a heart.

JOHN BUNYAN

There is no way that Christians, in a private
capacity, can do so much to promote the work of
God and advance the kingdom of Christ
as by prayer.

JONATHAN EDWARDS

MORE FROM GOD'S WORD

The LORD is far from the wicked but he hears
the prayer of the righteous.

PROVERBS 15:29 NIV

I want men everywhere to lift up holy hands
in prayer, without anger or disputing.

1 TIMOTHY 2:8 NIV

TODAY, WE WILL THINK ABOUT . . .

The role that prayer plays in the life of our family.

A PRAYER TO START OUR DAY

We pray to You, Father, because You desire it and
because we need it. Prayer not only changes things,
it changes us. Help us, Lord, never to face
the demands of the day without first
spending time with You. ~Amen

DAY 15

YOUR BEST FRIEND

A FRIEND LOVES YOU ALL THE TIME . . . .

PROVERBS 17:17 NCV.

D o you want your love to last forever? If so, here's a time-tested prescription for a blissfully happy marriage: make certain that your spouse is your best friend.

Genuine friendship between a husband and wife should be treasured and nurtured. As Christians, we are commanded to love one another. The familiar words of 1 Corinthians 13:2 remind us that love and charity are among God's greatest gifts: "And though I have the gift of prophecy, and understand all mysteries, and all knowledge; and though I have all faith, so that I could remove mountains, and have not charity, I am nothing" (KJV).

Is your spouse your best friend? If so, you are immensely blessed by God—never take this gift for granted. So today, remember the important role that friendship plays in your marriage. That friendship is, after all, a glorious gift, praised by God. Give thanks for that gift and nurture it.

Inasmuch as anyone pushes you nearer to God,
he or she is your friend.

BARBARA JOHNSON

We long to find someone who has been where
we've been, who shares our fragile skies,
who sees our sunsets with the same shades of blue.

BETH MOORE

When we honestly ask ourselves which person in
our lives means the most to us, we often find that it
is he who, instead of giving much advice, solutions,
and cures, has chosen rather to share our pain and
touch our wounds with a gentle and tender hand.
The friend who can be silent with us in a moment of
despair or confusion, who can stay with us in
an hour of grief and bereavement, who can tolerate
not knowing, not curing, not healing,
and face us with the reality of our powerlessness,
that is a friend who cares.

HENRI NOUWEN

MORE FROM GOD'S WORD

Greater love has no one than this,
that he lay down his life for his friends.

JOHN 15:13 NIV

As iron sharpens iron, a friend sharpens a friend.

PROVERBS 27:17 NLT

TODAY, WE WILL THINK ABOUT . . .

The role that friendship plays in our marriage.

A PRAYER TO START OUR DAY

We thank You, Lord, for the gift of marriage.
And we thank You for the love, the care,
the devotion, and the genuine friendship
that we share this day and forever. ~Amen

A GOLDEN RULE FOR TODAY . . . AND EVERY DAY

DO TO OTHERS WHAT YOU WANT THEM
TO DO TO YOU.

MATTHEW 7:12 NCV

The noted American theologian Phillips Brooks advised, "Be such a person, and live such a life, that if every person were such as you, and every life a life like yours, this earth would be God's Paradise." One tangible way to make your world a more godly place is to spread kindness wherever you go. And remember: kindness begins at home . . . but it should never end there.

For Christian couples, kindness is not an option; it is a commandment. Jesus teaches, "In everything, therefore, treat people the same way you want them to treat you, for this is the Law and the Prophets" (Matthew 7:12 NASB). Jesus did not say, "In some things, treat people as you wish to be treated." And, He did not say, "From time to time, treat others with kindness." Christ said that we should treat others as we wish to be treated in everything. This, of course, isn't always easy, but as Christians, we are commanded to do our best.

Today, as you consider all the things that Christ has done in your life, honor Him by being a little kinder than necessary. Honor Him by slowing down long enough to say an extra word of encouragement to your loved ones. Honor Him by picking up the phone and calling your spouse for no reason other than to say, "I'm thinking of you and I love you." Honor Christ by obeying the Golden Rule. He expects no less, and He deserves no less. And so, by the way, does your beloved.

~ ~ ~ ~ ~ ~ ~

It is wrong for anyone to be anxious to receive more from his neighbor than he himself is willing to give to God.

ST. FRANCIS OF ASSISI

Anything done for another is done for oneself.

POPE JOHN PAUL II

It is one of the most beautiful compensations of life that no one can sincerely try to help another without helping herself.

BARBARA JOHNSON

MORE FROM GOD'S WORD

Each of you should look not only to your own interests,
but also to the interest of others.

PHILIPPIANS 2:4 NIV

TODAY, WE WILL THINK ABOUT . . .

The importance of treating all people
with respect and kindness.

A PRAYER TO START OUR DAY

Dear Lord, we thank You for friends and family
members who practice the Golden Rule. Because
we expect to be treated with kindness, let us be
kind. Because we wish to be loved, let us be loving.
Because we need forgiveness, let us be merciful.
In matters great and small, let us live by the Golden
Rule, and let us express our gratitude to those
who offer kindness and generosity to us. ~Amen

DAY 17

DURING DIFFICULT DAYS

IN THIS WORLD YOU WILL HAVE TROUBLE.
BUT TAKE HEART!
I HAVE OVERCOME THE WORLD.

JOHN 16:33 NIV

From time to time, all of us face problems, disappointments, heartaches, and loss. Old Man Trouble pays periodic visits to each of us; none of us are exempt, and neither are our marriages. When we are troubled, God stands ready and willing to protect us. Our responsibility, of course, is to ask for His healing touch. When we call upon Him in heartfelt prayer, He will answer—in His own time and in accordance with His own perfect plan.

When we encounter problems or misunderstandings in our relationships, we must work to heal those problems sooner rather than later. Marital problems, like all problems, are most easily solved when they are new and small. That's why wise couples do the hard work of addressing their problems honestly, forthrightly, and quickly (even when they might prefer to downplay their difficulties or ignore those difficulties altogether).

Ignoring problems instead of fixing them is tempting but irresponsible. After all, if we won't solve our problems, who will? Or should?

In summary, the hallmark of a healthy marriage is not the absence of problems, but a willingness to solve those problems now. May you live—and love—accordingly.

We sometimes fear to bring our troubles to
God because we think they must seem small to Him.
But, if they are large enough to vex and endanger
our welfare, they are large enough to
touch His heart of love.

R. A. TORREY

Often the trials we mourn are really gateways
into the good things we long for.

HANNAH WHITALL SMITH

Looking back, I can see that the most exciting
events of my life have all risen out of trouble.

CATHERINE MARSHALL

Measure the size of the obstacles against
the size of God.

BETH MOORE

The truth is that even in the midst of trouble,
happy moments swim by us every day,
like shining fish waiting to be caught.

BARBARA JOHNSON

MORE FROM GOD'S WORD

*When troubles come and all these awful things
happen to you, in future days you will come back to
God, your God, and listen obediently to what he says.
God, your God, is above all a compassionate God.
In the end he will not abandon you, he won't
bring you to ruin, he won't forget the covenant
with your ancestors which he swore to them.*

DEUTERONOMY 4:30-31 MSG

TODAY, WE WILL THINK ABOUT . . .

The need to address our problems sooner
rather than later.

A PRAYER TO START OUR DAY

Lord, sometimes our problems are simply too big
for us, but they are never too big for You.
We will turn our troubles over to You, Lord,
and we will trust You today and
for all eternity. ~Amen

THE NEED FOR TRUST

GOOD PEOPLE WILL BE GUIDED BY HONESTY;
DISHONESTY WILL DESTROY THOSE
WHO ARE NOT TRUSTWORTHY.

PROVERBS 11:3 NCV

The best relationships—and the best marriages—are built upon a foundation of honesty and trust. Without trust, marriages soon begin to wither; with trust, marriages soon begin to flourish.

For Christians, honesty is the right policy because it's God's policy. God's Word makes it clear: "Lying lips are an abomination to the LORD, but those who deal truthfully are His delight" (Proverbs 12:22 NKJV).

Sometimes, honesty is difficult; sometimes, honesty is painful; sometimes, honesty makes us feel uncomfortable. Despite these temporary feelings of discomfort, we must make honesty the hallmark of all our relationships; otherwise, we invite needless suffering into our own lives and into the lives of those we love.

Do you want your love to last forever? Then you and your spouse must commit to build a relationship based upon mutual trust and unerring truth. Both of you deserve nothing less . . . and neither, for that matter, does God.

How committed are you to breaking the ice of
prayerlessness so that you and your mate can seek
the Lord openly and honestly together, releasing
control over your marriage into the capable,
trustworthy, but often surprising hands of God?

STORMIE OMARTIAN

Success, in a ministry or a marriage,
is not the key. Faithfulness is.

JONI EARECKSON TADA

Trust is like "money in the bank" in a marriage.
There must be a reasonable amount of it on deposit
to ensure the security of a marital union.

ED YOUNG

Integrity is not a given factor in everyone's life.
It is a result of self-discipline, inner trust,
and a decision to be relentlessly honest
in all situations in our lives.

JOHN MAXWELL

MORE FROM GOD'S WORD

The honest person will live in safety,
but the dishonest will be caught.

PROVERBS 10:9 NCV

Don't lie to one another. You're done with that old life.
It's like a filthy set of ill-fitting clothes you've stripped off
and put in the fire. Now you're dressed in
a new wardrobe. Every item of your new way of life is
custom-made by the Creator, with his label on it.
All the old fashions are now obsolete.

COLOSSIANS 3:9-10 MSG

TODAY, WE WILL THINK ABOUT . . .

The need for absolute trust in our marriage.

A PRAYER TO START OUR DAY

Heavenly Father, Your faithfulness is complete and
perfect. Help us to be faithful to You, dear Lord,
and help us be faithful to each other. ~Amen

DAY 19

SERVING TOGETHER

YOUR ATTITUDE SHOULD BE THE SAME AS
THAT OF CHRIST JESUS . . .
TAKING THE VERY NATURE OF A SERVANT.
PHILIPPIANS 2:5,7 NIV

As you and your spouse seek to discover God's unfolding plans for your family, you must ask yourself this question: "How does God want us to serve?"

Whatever your path, whatever your calling, you may be certain of this: service to others is an integral part of God's plan for you and your family. Christ was the ultimate servant, the Savior who gave His life for mankind. As His followers, we, too, must become humble servants in the service of our Lord.

Are you willing to become a humble servant for Christ? Are you willing to roll up your sleeves and do your part to make your corner of the world a better place to live? If you want to obey God, that's precisely what you must do.

As a humble servant, you will glorify yourself not before men, but before your Creator, and that's as it should be. After all, earthly glory is fleeting: here today and all too soon gone. But, heavenly glory endures throughout eternity. So, the choice is yours: Either you can lift yourself up here on earth and be humbled in heaven, or vice versa. Choose vice versa.

If we wish to make any progress in the service of
God, we must begin every day of our life
with new ardor.

CHARLES CARDINAL BORROMEO

Opportunities for service abound, and you will be
surprised that when you seek God's direction,
a place of suitable service will emerge where you can
express your love through service.

CHARLES STANLEY

You can judge how far you have risen in the scale
of life by asking one question: How wisely and
how deeply do I care? To be Christianized is to be
sensitized. Christians are people who care.

E. STANLEY JONES

If doing a good act in public will excite others to do
more good, then "Let your Light shine to all."
Miss no opportunity to do good.

JOHN WESLEY

MORE FROM GOD'S WORD

So prepare your minds for service and have self-control.

1 PETER 1:13 NCV

Whoever wants to become great among you must serve the rest of you like a servant.

MATTHEW 20:26 NCV

TODAY, WE WILL THINK ABOUT . . .

Creative ways that we can serve others.

A PRAYER TO START OUR DAY

Dear Lord, help us to be worthy servants to You and to Your children. When Jesus humbled Himself and became a servant, He also became an example for His followers. Make us faithful stewards of our gifts, and let us share our blessings with those in need. ~Amen

THE POWER OF PATIENCE

PATIENCE IS BETTER THAN PRIDE.

ECCLESIASTES 7:8 NLT

Loving relationships inevitably require patience . . . and lots of it! We live in an imperfect world inhabited by imperfect people, and we need to be patient with everybody, especially those we love. Most of us, however, are perfectly willing to be patient with our spouses just as long as things happen RIGHT NOW! Or sooner.

Ephesians 4:2 instructs us, "Be completely humble and gentle; be patient, bearing with one another in love" (NIV). But, for most of us, "bearing with one another" is difficult. Why? Because we are fallible human beings, sometimes quick to anger and sometimes slow to forgive.

The next time you find your patience tested to the limit, remember that the world unfolds according to God's timetable, not ours. Sometimes, we must wait patiently for our loved ones, and sometimes we must wait patiently for God. And that's as it should be. After all, think how patient God has been with us.

When we read of the great Biblical leaders,
we see that it was not uncommon for God to ask
them to wait, not just a day or two, but for years,
until God was ready for them to act.

GLORIA GAITHER

Let me encourage you to continue to wait
with faith. God may not perform a miracle,
but He is trustworthy to touch you and make you
whole where there used to be a hole.

LISA WHELCHEL

There is no such thing as a home completely
without conflicts. The last couple to live
"happily ever after" was Snow White and
Prince Charming. Even though you are committed
to your mate, there will still be times of tension,
tears, struggle, disagreement, and impatience.
Commitment doesn't erase our humanity!

CHARLES SWINDOLL

MORE FROM GOD'S WORD

And be careful that when you get on each other's nerves you don't snap at each other. Look for the best in each other, and always do your best to bring it out.

1 THESSALONIANS 5:15 MSG

Love is patient; love is kind.

1 CORINTHIANS 13:4 HCSB

TODAY, WE WILL THINK ABOUT . . .

The need to be patient, understanding, and compassionate.

A PRAYER TO START OUR DAY

Heavenly Father, give us patience. Let us live according to Your plan and according to Your timetable. When we are hurried, slow us down. When we become impatient with others, give us empathy. When we are frustrated by the demands of the day, give us peace. Today, let us be patient Christians, dear Lord, as we trust in You and in Your master plan for our lives. ~Amen

TRUSTING GOD'S PROMISES

WHEN GOD WANTED TO GUARANTEE
HIS PROMISES, HE GAVE HIS WORD,
A ROCK-SOLID GUARANTEE. GOD CAN'T
BREAK HIS WORD. AND BECAUSE HIS WORD
CANNOT CHANGE, THE PROMISE IS LIKEWISE
UNCHANGEABLE. IT'S AN UNBREAKABLE
SPIRITUAL LIFELINE, REACHING PAST
ALL APPEARANCES RIGHT TO
THE VERY PRESENCE OF GOD.

HEBREWS 6:17-19 MSG

I s your marriage built upon the foundation of God's promises? Hopefully so. A Christ-centered marriage is a joy to behold, a joy to experience, and a blessing forever.

A Christ-centered marriage is an exercise in faith, love, fidelity, trust, understanding, forgiveness, caring, sharing, and encouragement. It requires empathy, tenderness, patience, and perseverance. It is the union of two Christian adults, both of whom are willing to compromise and, when appropriate, to apologize. A Christ-centered marriage requires heaping helpings of common sense, common courtesy, and uncommon caring. It is a joy to behold, a joy to experience, and a blessing forever.

Does Christ truly preside over your marriage, or does He occupy a position of lesser importance? The answer to that question will determine the quality and direction of your marriage. When both you and your spouse allow Jesus to reign over your lives, Christ will bless you and your family in wonderful, unexpected ways. So today and every day, make your marriage a model of Christian love, respect, and service. Trust God's Word and expect Him to fulfill His promises. And rest assured: when you do your part, God will do His part.

The meaning of hope isn't just some flimsy wishing.
It's a firm confidence in God's promises—
that he will ultimately set things right.

SHEILA WALSH

A promise has credibility only in the capacity of
the person to guarantee it. God's character is
perfect, and he has the complete capacity to
guarantee any promise that He makes.

FRANKLIN GRAHAM

Claim all of God's promises in the Bible.
Your sins, your worries, your life—
you may cast them all on Him.

CORRIE TEN BOOM

In Biblical worship you do not find the repetition of
a phrase; instead, you find the worshipers rehearsing
the character of God and His ways, reminding Him
of His faithfulness and His wonderful promises.

KAY ARTHUR

Never doubt in the dark what God
told you in the light.

V. RAYMOND EDMAN

MORE FROM GOD'S WORD

*Whatever God has promised gets stamped with
the Yes of Jesus. In him, this is what we preach and
pray, the great Amen, God's Yes and our Yes together,
gloriously evident.*

2 CORINTHIANS 1:20 MSG

*Let us hold on to the confession of our hope without
wavering, for He who promised is faithful.*

HEBREWS 10:23 HCSB

TODAY, WE WILL THINK ABOUT . . .

God's faithfulness.

A PRAYER TO START OUR DAY

Heavenly Father, when we are troubled,
give us hope. When we are weak, give us strength.
When we are fearful, let us feel Your healing touch.
Let us trust in Your promises, Lord, and let us draw
strength from those promises and from
Your unending love. ~Amen

DAY 22

ABUNDANCE FOR YOU AND YOURS

I HAVE COME THAT THEY MAY HAVE LIFE,
AND THAT THEY MAY HAVE IT
MORE ABUNDANTLY.

JOHN 10:10 NKJV

The Word of God is clear: Christ came in order that we might have life abundant and life eternal. Eternal life is the priceless possession of all who invite Christ into their hearts, but God's abundance is optional: He does not force it upon us.

When we entrust our hearts and our days to the One who created us, we experience abundance through the grace and sacrifice of His Son. But, when we turn our thoughts and direct our energies away from God's commandments, we inevitably forfeit the spiritual abundance that might otherwise be ours.

God intends that the institution of marriage should be a continuing source of abundance for husbands and wives alike. But it's up to husbands and wives to claim God's abundance . . . or not.

Have you and your spouse accepted God's gift of abundance? If so, your marriage should reflect that decision. When you both honor God and obey Him without reservation, you both will receive the love and the abundance that He has promised.

Would you like a formula for a successful marriage? Seek first the kingdom of God and encourage your spouse to do likewise. Then, prepare yourselves for the joy, the peace, and the spiritual abundance that the Shepherd offers His sheep.

Instead of living a black-and-white existence,
we'll be released into a Technicolor world of
vibrancy and emotion when we more accurately
reflect His nature to the world around us.

BILL HYBELS

God loves you and wants you to experience
peace and life—abundant and eternal.

BILLY GRAHAM

People, places, and things were never meant
to give us life. God alone is the author
of a fulfilling life.

GARY SMALLEY & JOHN TRENT

We honor God by asking for great things when
they are a part of His promise. We dishonor Him
and cheat ourselves when we ask for molehills
where He has promised mountains.

VANCE HAVNER

MORE FROM GOD'S WORD

If you give, you will receive. Your gift will return to you in full measure, pressed down, shaken together to make room for more, and running over. Whatever measure you use in giving—large or small—it will be used to measure what is given back to you.

LUKE 6:38 NLT

TODAY, WE WILL THINK ABOUT . . .

The spiritual abundance that can be ours in Christ.

A PRAYER TO START OUR DAY

Heavenly Father, You have promised an abundant
life through Your Son Jesus. We thank You, Lord,
for Your abundance. Guide us according to
Your will, so that we might be worthy servants
in all that we say and do,
this day and every day. ~Amen

A TIME FOR RENEWAL

I WILL GIVE YOU A NEW HEART
AND PUT A NEW SPIRIT WITHIN YOU.

EZEKIEL 36:26 NKJV

Even the most inspired Christians can, from time to time, find themselves running on empty. The demands of daily life can drain us of our strength and rob us of the joy that is rightfully ours in Christ. When we find ourselves tired, discouraged, or worse, there is a source from which we can draw the power needed to recharge our spiritual batteries. That source is God.

God is in the business of making all things new, including marriages. When we feel the strains of everyday living tugging at the seams of our hearts, God is always able to renew us if we join together and ask Him to do so. Our obligation is to ask.

Are you and your spouse tired or troubled? Turn your hearts toward God in prayer. Are you weak or worried? Take the time—or, more accurately, make the time—to delve deeply into God's Holy Word. Are you spiritually depleted? Call upon fellow believers to support you, and call upon Christ to renew your marriage and your lives. When you do, you'll discover that the Creator of the universe stands ready to restore your strength, your relationship, and your love.

I wish I could make it all new again; I can't.
But God can. "He restores my soul,"
wrote the shepherd. God doesn't reform; he restores.
He doesn't camouflage the old; he restores the new.
The Master Builder will pull out the original plan
and restore it. He will restore the vigor;
he will restore the energy. He will restore the hope.
He will restore the soul.

MAX LUCADO

If the leaves had not been let go to fall and wither,
if the tree had not consented to be a skeleton for
many months, there would be no new life rising, no
bud, no flower, no fruit, no seed, no new generation.

ELISABETH ELLIOT

No matter how badly we have failed,
we can always get up and begin again.
Our God is the God of new beginnings.

WARREN WIERSBE

MORE FROM GOD'S WORD

*Therefore if anyone is in Christ,
he is a new creature; the old things passed away;
behold, new things have come.*

2 CORINTHIANS 5:17 HCSB

TODAY, WE WILL THINK ABOUT . . .

The strength that can be ours when we allow Christ
to dwell at the center of our marriage.

A PRAYER TO START OUR DAY

Heavenly Father, sometimes the demands of
the day leave us discouraged and frustrated.
Renew our strength, Father, and give us
patience and perspective. Let us live according to
Your Word, and let us grow in our faith
every day that we live. ~Amen

COMMUNICATION

A GENTLE ANSWER TURNS AWAY WRATH,
BUT A HARSH WORD STIRS UP ANGER.

PROVERBS 15:1 NIV

Your skills as a communicator will have a profound impact upon your relationships, starting with that most important relationship: your marriage. Here are a few simple rules that can help:

1. Think First, Speak Second: If you blurt out the first thing that comes into your head, you may say things that are better left unsaid.

2. Learn to Be a Good Listener: Far too many marriages are unsuccessful because one or both spouses simply don't make the effort to listen. If you want your marriage to flourish, listen carefully to your spouse.

3. Don't Be a Chronic Complainer: You'll never whine your way to a happy marriage, so don't even try.

4. Be a Trustworthy Communicator: Don't hedge the truth, don't omit important facts, and don't make promises that you can't keep.

5. Be Encouraging: You should be your spouse's biggest booster, not your spouse's constant critic.

Good communication is essential to a happy marriage. When you learn better ways to communicate with your spouse, your marriage will be blessed.

~ ~ ~ ~ ~ ~ ~

Part of good communication is listening with the eyes as well as with the ears.

JOSH MCDOWELL

Attitude and the spirit in which we communicate are as important as the words we say.

CHARLES STANLEY

We should ask ourselves three things before we speak: Is it true? Is it kind? Does it glorify God?

BILLY GRAHAM

MORE FROM GOD'S WORD

A wise person gets known for insight; gracious words add to one's reputation . . . . They make a lot of sense, these wise folks; whenever they speak, their reputation increases.

PROVERBS 16:21,23 MSG

A wise man's heart guides his mouth, and his lips promote instruction.

PROVERBS 16:23 NIV

TODAY, WE WILL THINK ABOUT . . .

The need to communicate honestly and often.

A PRAYER TO START OUR DAY

Dear Lord, You have warned us that we will be judged by the words we speak. Keep us mindful that we have influence on many people, and let the words that we speak today be worthy of the One who has saved us forever. ~Amen

A TIME TO ENCOURAGE

SO ENCOURAGE EACH OTHER AND
GIVE EACH OTHER STRENGTH.

1 THESSALONIANS 5:11 NCV

Marriage is a team sport, and all of us need occasional pats on the back from our teammate. In the Book of Proverbs, we read, "A word aptly spoken is like apples of gold in settings of silver" (25:11 NIV). This verse reminds us that the words we speak can and should be beautiful offerings to those we love.

All of us have the power to enrich the lives of our loved ones. Sometimes, when we feel uplifted and secure, we find it easy to speak words of encouragement and hope. Other times, when we are discouraged or tired, we can scarcely summon the energy to uplift ourselves, much less anyone else. But, as loving Christians, our obligation is clear: we must always measure our words carefully as we use them to benefit others and to glorify our Father in heaven.

God intends that we speak words of kindness, wisdom, and truth, no matter our circumstances, no matter our emotions. When we do, we share a priceless gift with our loved ones, and we give glory to the One who gave His life for us. As believers, we must do no less.

We do have the ability to encourage or
discourage each other with the words we say.
In order to maintain a positive mood,
our hearts must be in good condition.

ANNIE CHAPMAN

When we bring sunshine into the lives of others,
we're warmed by it ourselves.
When we spill a little happiness, it splashes on us.

BARBARA JOHNSON

Make it a rule, and pray to God to help you to keep
it, never to lie down at night without being able to
say: "I have made at least one human being a little
wiser, a little happier, or a little better this day."

CHARLES KINGSLEY

You have the power to lift your loved ones up or
to hold them back. When you learn how
to lift them up, you'll soon discover
that you've lifted yourself up, too.

CRISWELL FREEMAN

MORE FROM GOD'S WORD

Patience and encouragement come from God.
And I pray that God will help you all agree
with each other the way Christ Jesus wants.

ROMANS 15:5 NCV

Good people's words will help many others.

PROVERBS 10:21 NCV

TODAY, WE WILL THINK ABOUT . . .

The need to encourage each other.

A PRAYER TO START OUR DAY

Dear Heavenly Father, because we are Your
children, we are blessed. You have loved us eternally,
cared for us faithfully, and saved us through the
gift of Your Son Jesus. Just as You have lifted us up,
Lord, we will seek to lift each other up in a spirit of
encouragement, optimism, and hope. ~Amen

A WILLINGNESS TO PERSEVERE

THANKS BE TO GOD! HE GIVES US
THE VICTORY THROUGH OUR LORD
JESUS CHRIST. THEREFORE, MY DEAR
BROTHERS, STAND FIRM. LET NOTHING
MOVE YOU. ALWAYS GIVE YOURSELVES
FULLY TO THE WORK OF THE LORD,
BECAUSE YOU KNOW THAT YOUR LABOR
IN THE LORD IS NOT IN VAIN.

1 CORINTHIANS 15:57-58 NIV

Marriage is a marathon, not a sprint—and couples who expect otherwise will be sadly disappointed. That's why husbands and wives need large quantities of patience, forgiveness, hope, and perseverance.

Every marriage and every life has its share of roadblocks and stumbling blocks; these situations require courage and determination. As an example of perfect courage and steadfast determination, we need look no further than our Savior, Jesus Christ.

Jesus finished what He began. Despite the torture He endured, despite the shame of the cross, Jesus was steadfast in His faithfulness to God. We, too, must remain faithful—faithful to God, faithful to our principles, and faithful to our loved ones—especially during times of transition or hardship.

The next time you are tempted to give up on yourself, your duties, or your relationships, ask yourself this question: "What would Jesus have me do?" When you find the answer to *that* question, you'll know precisely what to do.

Let us not cease to do the utmost, that we may
incessantly go forward in the way of the Lord;
and let us not despair of the smallness
of our accomplishments.

JOHN CALVIN

Your life is not a boring stretch of highway.
It's a straight line to heaven. And just look at
the fields ripening along the way. Look at
the tenacity and endurance. Look at the grains
of righteousness. You'll have quite a crop
at harvest . . . so don't give up!

JONI EARECKSON TADA

Perseverance is more than endurance.
It is endurance combined with absolute assurance
and certainty that what we are looking for
is going to happen.

OSWALD CHAMBERS

Don't give up. Moses was once a basket case!

ANONYMOUS

MORE FROM GOD'S WORD

*Let us not lose heart in doing good, for in due time
we shall reap if we do not grow weary.
So then, while we have opportunity, let us do good
to all men, and especially to those
who are of the household of the faith.*

GALATIANS 6:9-10 NASB

TODAY, WE WILL THINK ABOUT . . .

The power of perseverance.

A PRAYER TO START OUR DAY

Dear Lord, when we are discouraged,
we will turn to You for strength, courage, and faith.
Today and every day, we will look to You as
the ultimate source of our hope, our strength,
our peace, and our salvation. ~Amen

GROWING TOGETHER

As newborn babies want milk, you should want the pure and simple teaching. By it you can grow up and be saved.

1 PETER 2:2 NCV

A Christian marriage can and should be a lifelong journey toward spiritual maturity and growth: as believers, we should never stop growing in the love and knowledge of our Savior.

When we cease to grow, either emotionally or spiritually, we do ourselves and our loved ones a profound disservice. But, if we study God's Word, if we obey His commandments, and if we live in the center of His will, we will not be "stagnant" believers; we will, instead, be growing Christians . . . and that's exactly what God wants for our marriages and our lives.

Many of life's most important lessons are painful to learn. Thankfully, during times of heartbreak and hardship, God stands ready to protect us. As Psalm 46:1 promises, "God is our protection and our strength. He always helps in times of trouble" (NCV). In His own time and according to His master plan, God will heal us if we invite Him into our hearts.

Spiritual growth need not take place only in times of adversity. We must seek to grow in our knowledge and love of the Lord every day that we live. In those quiet moments when we open our hearts to God, the One who made us keeps remaking us. He gives us direction, perspective, wisdom, and courage. And, the appropriate moment to accept those spiritual gifts is always the present one.

~ ~ ~ ~ ~ ~ ~

In reading the Bible, we study to know God,
to hear his voice, and to be changed by him
as we grow in holiness.

JAMES MONTGOMERY BOICE

God loves us the way we are,
but He loves us too much to leave us that way.

LEIGHTON FORD

With God, it isn't who you were that matters;
it's who you are becoming.

LIZ CURTIS HIGGS

MORE FROM GOD'S WORD

*So don't lose a minute in building on what
you've been given, complementing your basic faith with
good character, spiritual understanding, alert discipline,
passionate patience, reverent wonder, warm friendliness,
and generous love, each dimension fitting into and
developing the others.*

2 PETER 1:5-7 MSG

TODAY, WE WILL THINK ABOUT . . .

The fact that spiritual maturity is a journey,
not a destination.

A PRAYER TO START OUR DAY

Dear Lord, help us to keep growing spiritually
and emotionally. Let us live according to
Your Word, and let us grow in our faith
every day that we live. ~Amen

DAY 28

A DAY OF CELEBRATION

THIS IS THE DAY THE LORD HAS MADE.
WE WILL REJOICE AND BE GLAD IN IT.

PSALM 118:24 NLT

Christ made it clear to His followers: He intended that His joy would become their joy. And it still holds true today: Christ intends that His believers share His love with joy in their hearts. Yet sometimes, amid the inevitable hustle and bustle of life here on earth, we can forfeit—albeit temporarily—the joy of Christ as we wrestle with the challenges of daily living.

Joy is an important part of healthy Christian relationships. Joyful believers tend to form joyful relationships, and that is exactly what God intends.

C. H. Spurgeon, the renowned 19th-century English clergyman, advised, "The Lord is glad to open the gate to every knocking soul. It opens very freely; its hinges are not rusted; no bolts secure it. Have faith and enter at this moment through holy courage. If you knock with a heavy heart, you shall yet sing with joy of spirit. Never be discouraged!"

Are you doing your best to live each day as a joyful servant of Christ? And, are you inviting your spouse to join in the celebration? Hopefully so. After all, few things in life are more wonderful to behold than the joining together of two joyful believers. So now, with no further ado, thank God for your marriage, and let the celebration begin!

If you can forgive the person you were,
accept the person you are, and believe in
the person you will become, you are headed for joy.
So celebrate your life.

BARBARA JOHNSON

Celebration is possible only through the deep
realization that life and death are never found
completely separate. Celebration can really come
about only where fear and love, joy and sorrow,
tear and smiles can exist together.

HENRI NOUWEN

Some of us seem so anxious about avoiding hell that
we forget to celebrate our journey toward heaven.

PHILIP YANCEY

All our life is a celebration for us; we are convinced,
in fact, that God is always everywhere.
We sing while we work . . . we pray while we
carry out all life's other occupations.

ST. CLEMENT OF ALEXANDRIA

MORE FROM GOD'S WORD

Celebrate God all day, every day. I mean, revel in him!
PHILIPPIANS 4:4 MSG

Rejoice always; pray without ceasing.
2 THESSALONIANS 5:16-17 NASB

TODAY, WE WILL THINK ABOUT . . .

The need to celebrate our family and our marriage.

A PRAYER TO START OUR DAY

Lord, You are the Giver of all life, and
You have created us to have fellowship with You.
Let us live our lives in ways that are pleasing to You.
We will celebrate together, Father, and we will
give thanks for Your blessings today and
throughout all eternity. ~Amen

WALKING IN HIS FOOTSTEPS

AND WHEN HE HAD SPOKEN THIS,
HE SAID TO HIM, "FOLLOW ME."

JOHN 21:19 NKJV

I s your marriage built upon the solid foundation of God's love? Do you strive to be obedient to Him as you follow in the footsteps of His only begotten Son? If so, you are the recipient of countless blessings from the Father above. If not, it's time to reconsider your priorities for your marriage and your life.

When you and your spouse accept God's love with open arms, you are forever changed. When you embrace God's love, you will be blessed and protected . . . now and forever.

God understands your hopes, your fears, and your temptations. He understands what it means to be angry and what it costs to forgive. He knows the heart, the conscience, and the soul of every person who has ever lived, including you. And God has a plan of salvation that is intended for you. Accept it. Accept God's gift through the person of His Son Christ Jesus, and then rest assured: God walked among us so that you might have eternal life; amazing though it may seem, He did it for you.

The man who walks with God always gets
to his destination.

HENRIETTA MEARS

As a child of God, rest in the knowledge that
your Savior precedes you, and He will walk with
you through each experience of your life.

HENRY BLACKABY

Approach the Scriptures not so much as a manual of
Christian principles but as the testimony of
God's friends on what it means to walk with him
through a thousand different episodes.

JOHN ELDREDGE

Walking with God down the avenue of prayer,
we acquire something of His likeness, and
unconsciously we become witnesses to others of
His beauty and His grace.

E. M. BOUNDS

Think of this—we may live together with Him
here and now, a daily walking with Him
who loved us and gave Himself for us.

ELISABETH ELLIOT

MORE FROM GOD'S WORD

*And what does the L*ORD *require of you? To act justly and to love mercy and to walk humbly with your God.*

MICAH 6:8 NIV

TODAY, WE WILL THINK ABOUT

Following Christ Is a Daily Journey: When you decide to walk in the footsteps of the Master, that means that you're agreeing to be a disciple seven days a week, not just on Sunday. Remember the words of Vance Havner: "We must live in all kinds of days, both high days and low days, in simple dependence upon Christ as the branch on the vine. This is the supreme experience."

A PRAYER TO START OUR DAY

Dear Lord, each day we will walk with You. As we walk together, we pray that Your presence will be reflected in our lifes, and that Your love will dwell within our hearts this day and every day. ~Amen

LOVE THAT LASTS FOREVER

WE KNOW HOW MUCH GOD LOVES US,
AND WE HAVE PUT OUR TRUST IN HIM.
GOD IS LOVE, AND ALL WHO LIVE IN LOVE
LIVE IN GOD, AND GOD LIVES IN THEM.

1 JOHN 4:16 NLT

The Bible makes it clear that God's love for you and your spouse is deeper and more profound than either of you can imagine.

When you and your spouse embrace God together, both of you are forever changed. When you embrace God's love, you feel differently about yourself, your marriage, your family, and your world. When you join together and accept God's love, the two of you will be transformed.

So, if you and your mate genuinely want to build a love that endures, make God the focus of your marriage. When you do, your marriage will last forever—and so will your love.

When did God's love for you begin?
When He began to be God.
When did He begin to be God?
Never, for He has always been without
beginning and without end,
and so He has always loved you from eternity.

ST. FRANCIS OF SALES

As you are married through the years,
you can keep on falling in love—
over and over again.

ED YOUNG

The love life of the Christian is
a crucial battleground. There, if nowhere else,
it will be determined who is Lord: the world,
the self, and the devil—or the Lord Christ.

ELISABETH ELLIOT

A man and woman should choose each other for
life for the simple reason that a long life is barely
enough time for a man and woman to understand
each other, and to understand is to love.

GEORGE TRUETT

MORE FROM GOD'S WORD

*Love never ends. There are gifts of prophecy,
but they will be ended. There are gifts of speaking
in different languages, but those gifts will stop.
There is the gift of knowledge, but it will come to
an end. The reason is that our knowledge and our ability
to prophesy are not perfect. But when perfection comes,
the things that are not perfect will end.*

1 CORINTHIANS 13:8-10 NCV

TODAY, WE WILL THINK ABOUT . . .

Love that endures forever.

A PRAYER TO START OUR DAY

Thank You, Lord, for Your love. Your love is
boundless, infinite, and eternal. Today, let us pause
and reflect upon Your love for us, and let us share
that love with all those who cross our paths.
And, as an expression of our love for You, Father,
let us share the saving message of Your Son with
a world in desperate need of His peace. ~Amen

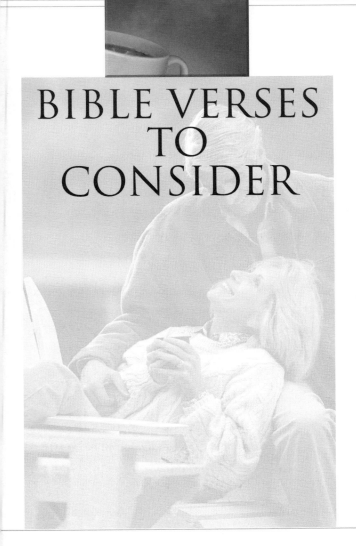

BIBLE VERSES
TO
CONSIDER

KINDNESS

*And be ye kind one to another, tenderhearted,
forgiving one another, even as God for Christ's sake
hath forgiven you.*

EPHESIANS 4:32 KJV

*Carry each other's burdens, and in this way
you will fulfill the law of Christ.*

GALATIANS 6:2 NIV

*Our Father is kind; you be kind. "Don't pick on people,
jump on their failures, criticize their faults—unless,
of course, you want the same treatment. Don't condemn
those who are down; that hardness can boomerang.
Be easy on people; you'll find life a lot easier."*

LUKE 6:36-37 MSG

*I tell you the truth, anything you did
for even the least of my people here, you also did for me.*

MATTHEW 25:40 NCV

FINALLY, ALL OF YOU
BE OF ONE MIND,
HAVING COMPASSION FOR
ONE ANOTHER; LOVE AS BROTHERS,
BE TENDERHEARTED,
BE COURTEOUS.

1 PETER 3:8 NKJV

WORSHIP

Happy are those who hear the joyful call to worship,
for they will walk in the light of your presence, LORD.

PSALM 89:15 NLT

All the earth shall worship You and sing praises to You;
They shall sing praises to Your name.

PSALM 66:4 NKJV

God lifted him high and honored him far beyond anyone
or anything, ever, so that all created beings in heaven
and earth, even those long ago dead and buried,
will bow in worship before this Jesus Christ,
and call out in praise that he is the Master of all,
to the glorious honor of God the Father.

PHILIPPIANS 2:9-11 MSG

God is spirit, and those who worship him
must worship in spirit and truth.

JOHN 4:24 NCV

WORSHIP THE LORD YOUR GOD AND
. . . SERVE HIM ONLY.

MATTHEW 4:10 HCSB

LAUGHTER

Shout for joy to the LORD, all the earth,
burst into jubilant song with music; make music
to the LORD with the harp, with the harp and
the sound of singing, with trumpets and
the blast of the ram's horn—shout for joy
before the LORD, the King.

PSALM 98:4-6 NIV

A cheerful heart is good medicine.

PROVERBS 17:22 NIV

. . . as the occasion when Jews got relief from
their enemies, the month in which their sorrow turned to
joy, mourning somersaulted into a holiday for parties and
fun and laughter, the sending and receiving of
presents and of giving gifts to the poor.

ESTHER 9:22 MSG

There is a time for everything, and everything
on earth has its special season . . . .
There is a time to cry and a time to laugh.
There is a time to be sad and a time to dance.

ECCLESIASTES 3:1, 4 NCV

LAUGH WITH YOUR HAPPY FRIENDS
WHEN THEY'RE HAPPY;
SHARE TEARS WHEN THEY'RE DOWN.

ROMANS 12:15 MSG

WORRY

When my anxious thoughts multiply within me,
Your consolations delight my soul.

PSALM 94:19 NASB

Don't fret or worry. Instead of worrying, pray.
Let petitions and praises shape your worries into prayers,
letting God know your concerns. Before you know it,
a sense of God's wholeness, everything coming together
for good, will come and settle you down.
It's wonderful what happens when Christ displaces
worry at the center of your life.

PHILIPPIANS 4:6-7 MSG

Therefore I tell you, do not worry about your life,
what you will eat or drink; or about your body,
what you will wear. Is not life more important
than food, and the body more important than clothes?
Look at the birds of the air; they do not sow or reap or
store away in barns, and yet your heavenly Father
feeds them. Are you not much more valuable than they?

MATTHEW 6:25-27 NIV

So don't worry about tomorrow,
for tomorrow will bring
its own worries.
Today's trouble
is enough for today.

Matthew 6:34 nlt

MONEY

For the love of money is the root of all evil.

1 TIMOTHY 6:10 KJV

Keep your lives free from the love of money,
and be satisfied with what you have.

HEBREWS 13:5 NCV

No one can serve two masters. For you will hate one
and love the other, or be devoted to one and despise
the other. You cannot serve both God and money.

LUKE 16:13 NLT

Trust in your money and down you go!
But the godly flourish like leaves in spring.

PROVERBS 11:28 NLT

If riches increase, do not set your heart upon them.

PSALM 62:10 NASB

WORK

Whatever your hand finds to do, do it with your might.
ECCLESIASTES 9:10 NKJV

Indolence wants it all and gets nothing;
the energetic have something to show for their lives.
PROVERBS 13:4 MSG

Do not be lazy but work hard,
serving the Lord with all your heart.
ROMANS 12:11 NCV

Those who work their land will have plenty of food,
but the ones who chase empty dreams
instead will end up poor.
PROVERBS 28:19 NCV

We want each of you to go on with the same hard work
all your lives so you will surely get what you hope for.
We do not want you to become lazy.
Be like those who through faith and patience
will receive what God has promised.
HEBREWS 6:11-12 NCV

OBEDIENCE

Therefore, get your minds ready for action,
being self-disciplined, and set your hope completely
on the grace to be brought to you at the revelation of
Jesus Christ. As obedient children, do not be conformed
to the desires of your former ignorance but,
as the One who called you is holy,
you also are to be holy in all your conduct.

1 PETER 1:13-15 HCSB

Does the LORD delight in burnt offerings and sacrifices as
much as in obeying the voice of the LORD?
To obey is better than sacrifice . . . .

1 SAMUEL 15:22 NIV

We must obey God rather than men.

ACTS 5:29 NASB

By faith Abraham, when called to go to a place he would
later receive as his inheritance, obeyed and went,
even though he did not know where he was going.

HEBREWS 11:8 NIV

THE WORLD AND ITS DESIRES
PASS AWAY, BUT THE MAN
WHO DOES THE WILL OF GOD
LIVES FOREVER.

1 JOHN 2:17 NIV

WITNESSING

You are the light of the world. A city situated on a hill
cannot be hidden. No one lights a lamp and puts it under
a basket, but rather on a lampstand, and it gives light for
all who are in the house. In the same way, let your light
shine before men, so that they may see your good works
and give glory to your Father in heaven.

MATTHEW 5:14-16 HCSB

But when the Holy Spirit has come upon you,
you will receive power and will tell people about
me everywhere—in Jerusalem, throughout Judea,
in Samaria, and to the ends of the earth.

ACTS 1:8 NLT

God's servant must not be argumentative,
but a gentle listener and a teacher who keeps cool,
working firmly but patiently with those who refuse
to obey. You never know how or when God
might sober them up with a change of heart
and a turning to the truth.

2 TIMOTHY 2:24-25 MSG

AND I SAY TO YOU,
ANYONE WHO ACKNOWLEDGES ME
BEFORE MEN, THE SON OF MAN
WILL ALSO ACKNOWLEDGE HIM
BEFORE THE ANGELS OF GOD;
BUT WHOEVER DENIES ME BEFORE
MEN WILL BE DENIED BEFORE
THE ANGELS OF GOD.

LUKE 12:8-9 HCSB

OPTIMISM

I can do everything through him that gives me strength.

PHILIPPIANS 4:13 NIV

For God has not given us a spirit of fear,
but of power and of love and of a sound mind.

2 TIMOTHY 1:7 NLT

My cup runs over. Surely goodness and
mercy shall follow me all the days of my life;
and I will dwell in the house of the LORD Forever.

PSALM 23:5-6 NKJV

But we are hoping for something we do not have yet,
and we are waiting for it patiently.

ROMANS 8:25 NCV

MAKE ME TO HEAR
JOY AND GLADNESS.

PSALM 51:8 KJV

PARENTING

Parents, don't come down too hard on your children or you'll crush their spirits.

COLOSSIANS 3:20 MSG

Fathers, do not provoke your children to anger, but bring them up in the discipline and instruction of the Lord.

EPHESIANS 6:4 NASB

Train up a child in the way he should go: and when he is old, he will not depart from it.

PROVERBS 22:6 KJV

God-loyal people, living honest lives, make it much easier for their children.

PROVERBS 20:7 MSG

THE GODLY WALK WITH INTEGRITY;
BLESSED ARE THEIR CHILDREN
AFTER THEM.

PROVERBS 20:7 NLT

TODAY

*For he says, "In the time of my favor I heard you,
and in the day of salvation I helped you."
I tell you, now is the time of God's favor,
now is the day of salvation.*

2 CORINTHIANS 6:2 NIV

*Since everything here today might well be
gone tomorrow, do you see how essential it is
to live a holy life?*

2 PETER 3:11 MSG

Encourage one another daily, as long as it is Today . . . .

HEBREWS 3:13 NIV

*Give your entire attention to what God is doing
right now, and don't get worked up about what may or
may not happen tomorrow. God will help you deal with
whatever hard things come up when the time comes.*

MATTHEW 6:34 MSG

I KNOW WHOM I HAVE BELIEVED,
AND AM CONVINCED THAT HE IS
ABLE TO GUARD WHAT I HAVE
ENTRUSTED TO HIM FOR THAT DAY.

2 TIMOTHY 1:12 NIV

PASSION

He did it with all his heart. So he prospered.

2 CHRONICLES 31:21 NKJV

In all the work you are doing,
work the best you can.
Work as if you were doing it for the Lord,
not for people.

COLOSSIANS 3:23 NCV

I have seen that there is nothing better than
for a person to enjoy his activities,
because that is his reward.
For who can enable him to see
what will happen after he dies?

ECCLESIASTES 3:22 HCSB

Whatever work you do, do your best,
because you are going to the grave,
where there is no working . . . .

ECCLESIASTES 9:10 NCV

NEVER BE LACKING IN ZEAL,
BUT KEEP YOUR SPIRITUAL FERVOR,
SERVING THE LORD.

ROMANS 12:11 NIV

THOUGHTS

*Do not conform any longer to the pattern of this world,
but be transformed by the renewing of your mind.
Then you will be able to test and approve what
God's will is—his good, pleasing and perfect will.*

ROMANS 12:2 NIV

*Be careful what you think,
because your thoughts run your life.*

PROVERBS 4:23 NCV

*Fix your thoughts on what is true and honorable
and right. Think about things that are pure and lovely
and admirable. Think about things that are
excellent and worthy of praise.*

PHILIPPIANS 4:8 NLT

*Those who are pure in their thinking are happy,
because they will be with God.*

MATTHEW 5:8 NCV

MAY THE WORDS OF MY MOUTH AND
THE THOUGHTS OF MY HEART BE
PLEASING TO YOU, O LORD,
MY ROCK AND MY REDEEMER.

PSALM 19:14 NLT

TRUTH

These are the things you are to do:
Speak the truth to each other, and render true
and sound judgment in your courts . . . .

ZECHARIAH 8:16 NIV

Teach me Your way, O LORD;
I will walk in Your truth.

PSALM 86:11 NASB

Buy the truth and do not sell it;
get wisdom, discipline, and understanding.

PROVERBS 23:23 NIV

And you shall know the truth,
and the truth shall make you free.

JOHN 8:32 NKJV

BUT WHEN THE SPIRIT
OF TRUTH COMES,
HE WILL LEAD YOU INTO ALL TRUTH.

JOHN 16:13 NCV

THANKSGIVING

Come, let us sing to the LORD!
Let us give a joyous shout to the rock of our salvation!
Let us come before him with thanksgiving.
Let us sing him psalms of praise.

PSALM 95:1-2 NLT

All Your works shall give thanks to You, O LORD,
And Your godly ones shall bless You.

PSALM 145:10 NASB

Enter his gates with thanksgiving; go into his courts
with praise. Give thanks to him and bless his name.
For the LORD is good. His unfailing love continues
forever, and his faithfulness continues to
each generation.

PSALM 100:4-5 NLT

And let the peace of God rule in your hearts,
to which also you were called in one body;
and be thankful.

COLOSSIANS 3:15 NKJV

IS ANYONE HAPPY?
LET HIM SING SONGS OF PRAISE.

JAMES 5:13 NIV